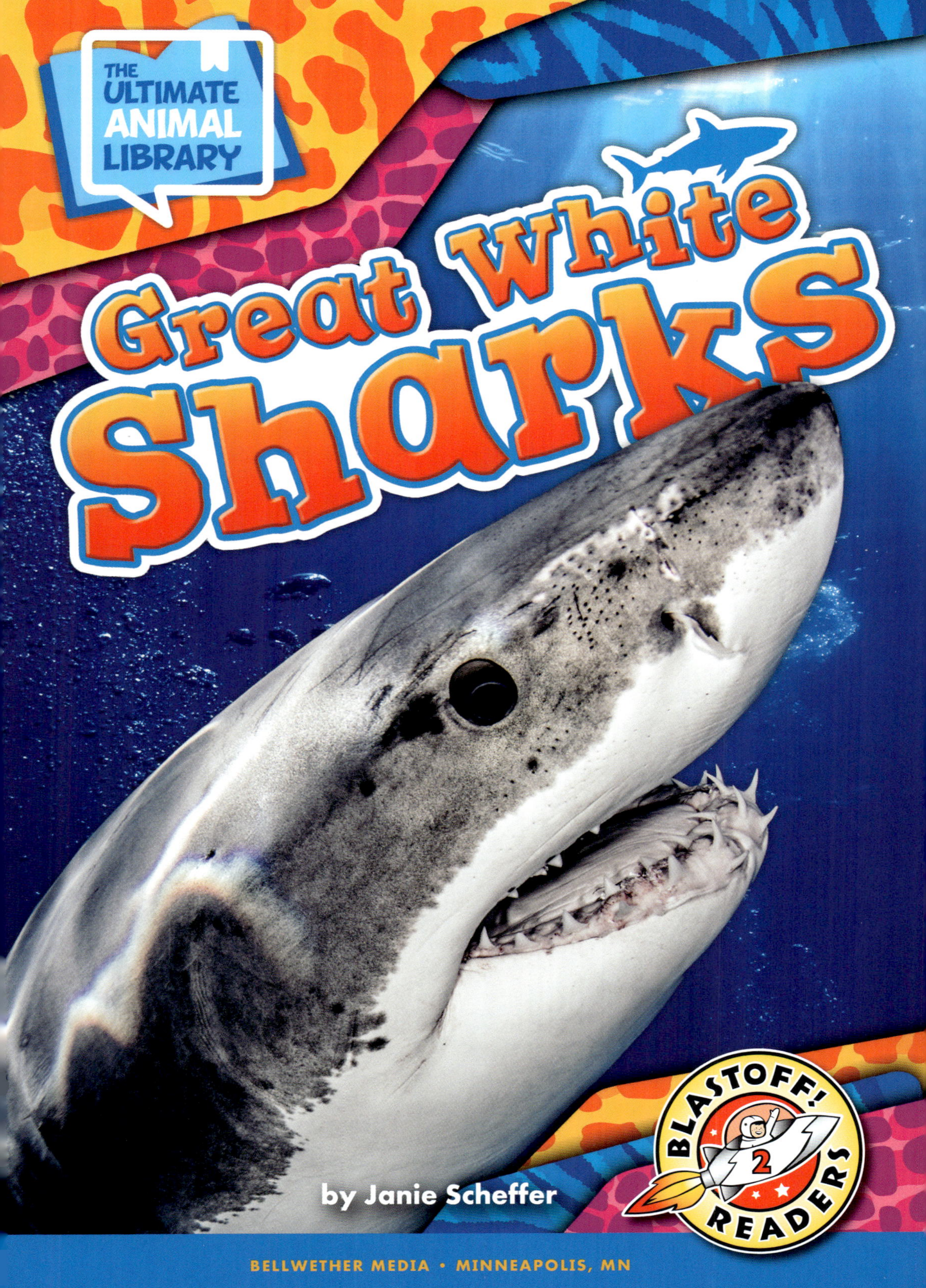
THE ULTIMATE ANIMAL LIBRARY
Great White Sharks
by Janie Scheffer
BLASTOFF! READERS
2
BELLWETHER MEDIA • MINNEAPOLIS, MN

Blastoff! Readers are carefully developed by literacy experts to build reading stamina and move students toward fluency by combining standards-based content with developmentally appropriate text.

Level 1 provides the most support through repetition of high-frequency words, light text, predictable sentence patterns, and strong visual support.

Level 2 offers early readers a bit more challenge through varied sentences, increased text load, and text-supportive special features.

Level 3 advances early-fluent readers toward fluency through increased text load, less reliance on photos, advancing concepts, longer sentences, and more complex special features.

★ **Blastoff! Universe**

Reading Level

Grade
K

Grades
1–3

Grade
4

This edition first published in 2025 by Bellwether Media, Inc.

Library of Congress Cataloging-in-Publication Data

Names: Scheffer, Janie, 1992- author.
Title: Great white sharks / by Janie Scheffer.
Description: Minneapolis, MN : Bellwether Media, Inc., [2025] | Series: The ultimate animal library | Includes bibliographical references and index. | Audience: Ages 5-8 | Audience: Grades 2-3 | Summary: "Relevant images match informative text in this introduction to Great white sharks. Intended for students in kindergarten through third grade"-- Provided by publisher.
Identifiers: LCCN 2024038362 (print) | LCCN 2024038363 (ebook) | ISBN 9798893042405 (library binding) | ISBN 9798893043372 (ebook)
Subjects: LCSH: White shark--Juvenile literature. | White shark--Life cycles--Juvenile literature.
Classification: LCC QL638.95.L3 S34 2025 (print) | LCC QL638.95.L3 (ebook) | DDC 597.3/3--dc23/eng/20240911
LC record available at https://lccn.loc.gov/2024038362
LC ebook record available at https://lccn.loc.gov/2024038363

Editor: Elizabeth Neuenfeldt   Series Designer: Veah Demmin

Printed in the United States of America, North Mankato, MN.

Table of Contents

What Are Great White Sharks?

Great white sharks are huge fish. They have around 300 teeth! These fish live in oceans around the world.

Great White Shark Report

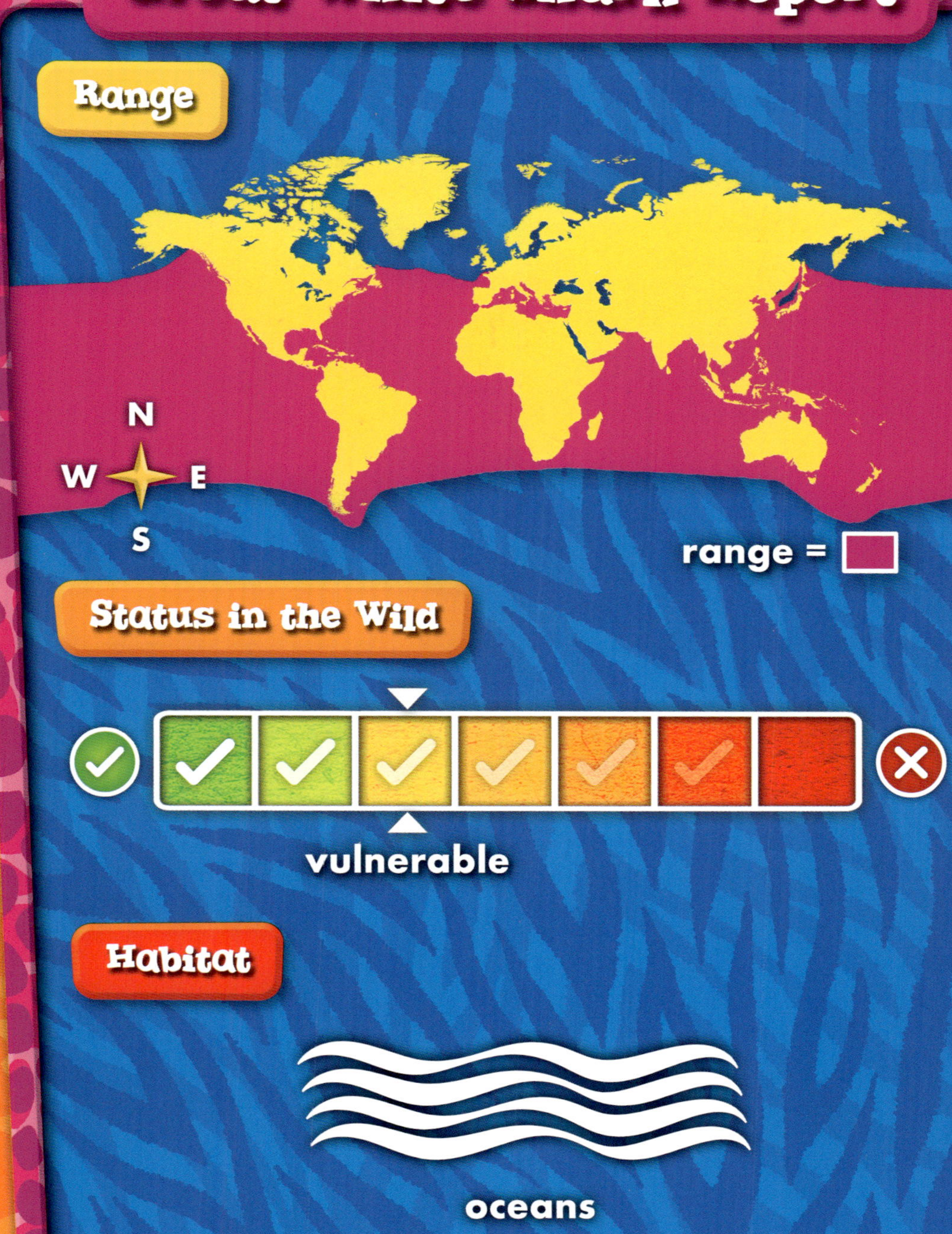

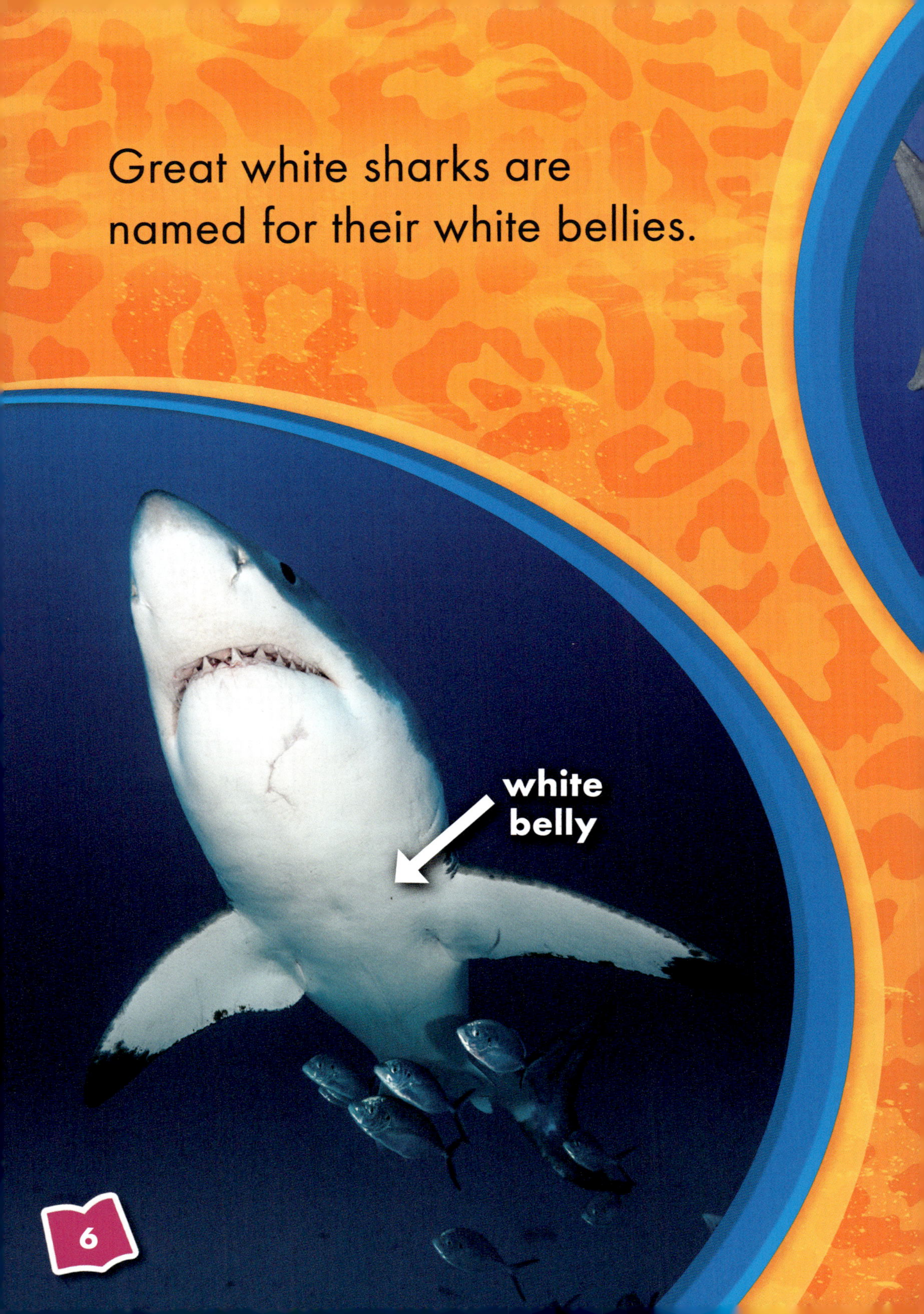

Great white sharks are named for their white bellies.

Their topsides can be blue, gray, or brown. Their colors help them hide while they hunt.

Great white sharks are the largest **predatory** fish. They can weigh up to 4,500 pounds (2,041 kilograms).

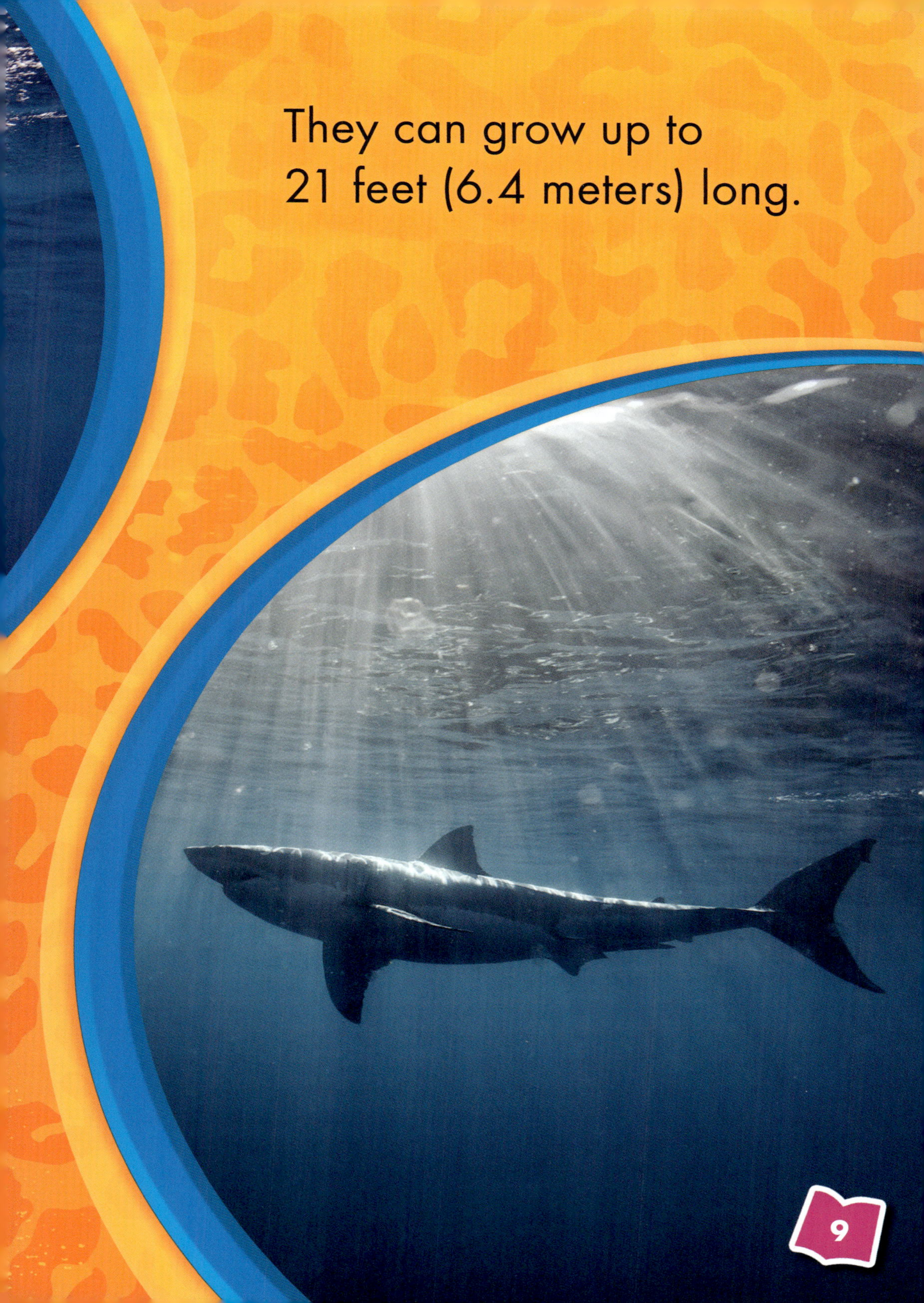

They can grow up to
21 feet (6.4 meters) long.

Great white sharks are **torpedo-shaped**. They have pointed **snouts**. Their curved tail fins are powerful.

Their shape helps them swim fast. They swim up to 35 miles (56 kilometers) per hour!

torpedo-shaped body

curved tail fin

pointed snout

white belly

Powerful Bites!

Great white sharks mostly live alone. Many live in feeding areas near coasts.

Some **migrate** into open oceans.

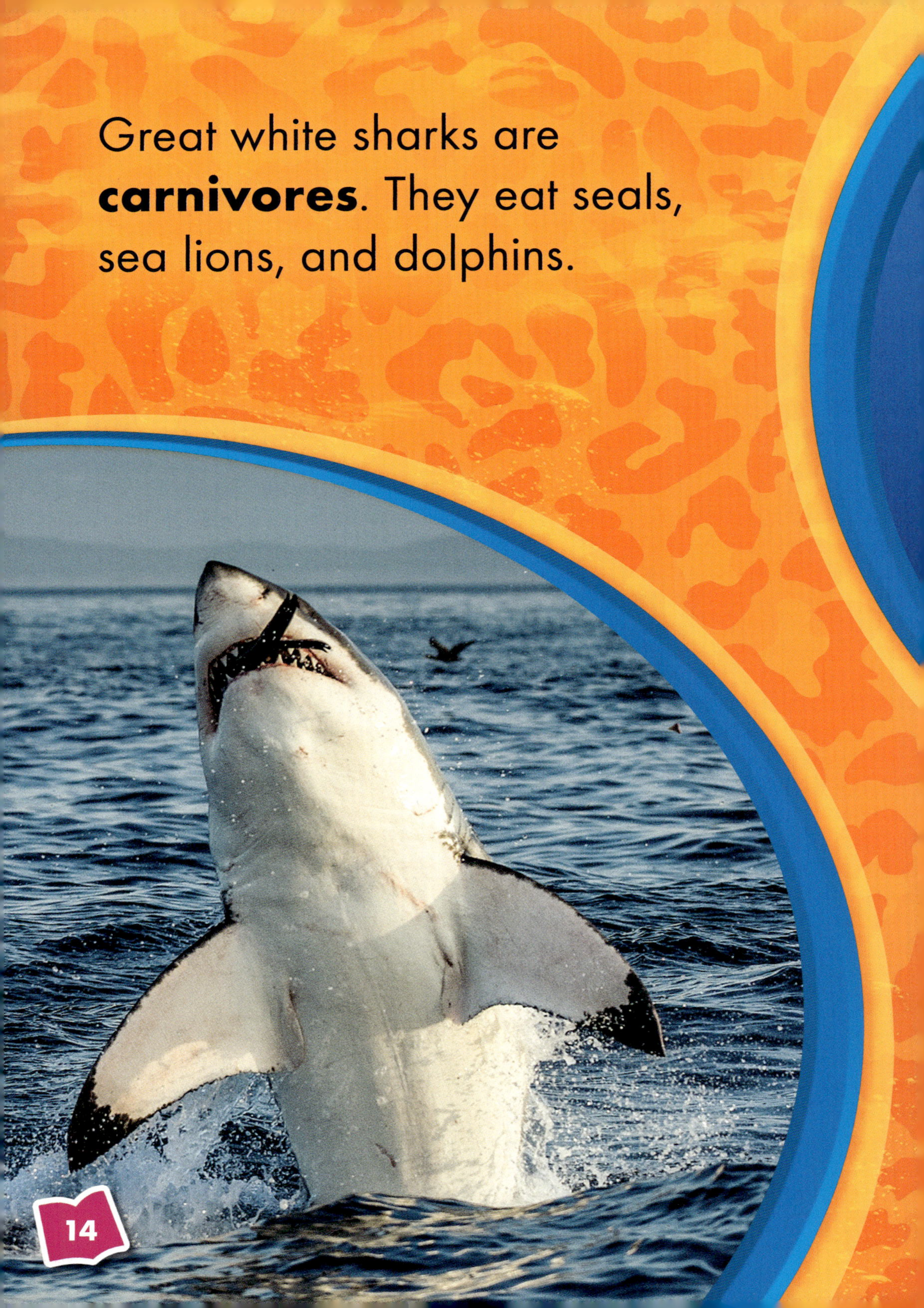

Great white sharks are **carnivores**. They eat seals, sea lions, and dolphins.

They also eat fish
and small whales.

Great white sharks **ambush** their **prey**. First, they swim beneath their meal.

Then they quickly swim up and bite into it!

Growing Up

Female great white sharks give birth to a **litter**. Each litter has 2 to 17 **pups**.

Pups can be 4 to 6 feet (1.2 to 1.8 meters) long at birth.

pup

Pups are born ready to live on their own. They can swim and hunt right away.

These mighty predators can live to be 70 years old!

Name of Babies

pups

Number of Babies

2 to 17

Time Spent with Mom

Life Span

Glossary

ambush—to hunt by lying in wait

carnivores—animals that only eat meat

litter—a group of baby sharks born at the same time

migrate—to travel from one place to another, often with the seasons

predatory—relating to animals that hunt other animals for food

prey—animals that are hunted by other animals for food

pups—baby great white sharks

snouts—the noses and mouths of some animals

torpedo-shaped—having a tube shape like a torpedo; torpedoes are weapons fired underwater.

To Learn More

AT THE LIBRARY

Musgrave, Ruth A. *Great White Sharks.* New York, N.Y.: DK Publishing, 2023.

Schuh, Mari. *Great White Sharks.* Minneapolis, Minn.: Jump!, 2024.

Storm, Marysa. *Great White Sharks*. Mankato, Minn.: Black Rabbit Books, 2024.

ON THE WEB

FACTSURFER

Factsurfer.com gives you a safe, fun way to find more information.

1. Go to www.factsurfer.com.
2. Enter "great white sharks" into the search box and click 🔍.
3. Select your book cover to see a list of related content.

Index

The images in this book are reproduced through the courtesy of: Image Source Trading Ltd, front cover; Willyam Bradberry, front cover background, interior background, p. 9; GermanVectorPro, front cover (shark icon); Steve Hinczynski, p. 3; Andrea Izzotti, p. 4; wildestanimal, p. 6; Julian Gunther, p. 7; Image Source/ Getty Images, p. 8; Jsegalexplore, pp. 10, 19, 20; Alastair Pollock Photography/ Getty Images, pp. 10-11; Scupix, p. 11; Sergey Uryadnikov, pp. 12, 14; Ramon Carretero, p. 13; vladoskan, p. 15; Jennifer Mellon Photos, pp. 16-17; Roberto 33, p. 17 (shark); Stuedal, p. 17 (seals); Nick Pecker, p. 17 (sea lions); Nicolas-SB, p. 17 (dolphins); Longjourneys, p. 18; Education Images/ Universal Images Group/ Getty Images, p. 21; Fiona Ayerst, p. 23.